Tree Bark

Lance R. Higgins

Edited by:
Aaron Lelito and Martha Sprackland

Copyright © 2024 Lance R. Higgins
All rights reserved.
ISBN: 979-8-9902815-1-6

Mom, *Dad*, and *Sis*, I love you. Thank you for supporting me.

Thank you to everyone who brought me relief.

Jess, thank you for becoming my little bee.

For those who are still growing.

Contents

Prelude..7

Part I: Ravaged Roots..........................13

Part II: Burrowing Beetles..................27

Part III: Falling Leaves.......................45

Part IV: Silent Ascent.........................63

Part V: Aubade....................................81

Prelude

I rarely read introductions, but after writing mine, I realize how important they actually are. I originally wanted my introduction to feel foreboding. I wanted my introduction to feel stoic. I spent so much time thinking about how I was going to write an introduction that felt just as important as the collection. I asked myself many questions: *Do I make it seem deep and full of thought? Do I get to the point or talk lengthily about my poems? Are people even going to read my introduction?*

Now that I have finally finished my collection after all these years, I know I want my introduction to simply feel *sincere*. Instead of writing my introduction with words and sentences that match my "writing voice," I decided to write the words of my introduction as I would say them aloud.

The next section isn't a happy dive into the how and why, but it's necessary so I can explain how I arrived in vast fields of bliss and happiness.

~ ~ ~

I could start talking about how worried I was when my dad was hospitalized for heart issues. I could talk about how worried I was when an armed F-16 crashed through the warehouse my mom was working in just a week later. I could talk about the way I lost three dogs, Lola, Rex, and

Sadie, to cancer or other fatal means. I could talk about how I lost a fatherly figure, Richard, to cancer. I could talk about how our long-time friend, Julie, who allowed my family to rent our home rather cheaply, was diagnosed with cancer. (Yes, I noticed the pattern forming that year, too. By the way, all of those were *before* COVID-19 had us in lockdown. It was quite the year before the storm.) I have to start somewhere, though, so I'll start where I feel my story officially began: April 5th, 2019.

    This was the day I broke up with a girl I dated for almost four years. I found love for the first time with her. I can say I loved her with my soul and with an intensity I believed would never fade, but it did as clarity pushed through the abuse. You always hear about the way heartbreak destroys you, but I never expected it to bring out the worst in me. I struggled for years to heal. When people talk about heartbreak, they sugarcoat how numb you can become. Heartbreak feels like your soul ran out of your body and left you behind with no way to hold love in your heart. Heartbreak makes the quiet of your mind scream louder than the ringing you hear in a dead-silent room. Your mind wanders in a state of untethered emotional vacancy. I couldn't stand constantly sitting in my silence, suffering quietly. I couldn't keep acting like I was okay every day. My numbness drifted into feelings of anger and confusion. I started writing long, disorderly paragraphs to try and cope with the loss and heartbreak. The paragraphs evolved into stanzas. The stanzas became lyrics. After enough time, writing poetry became my way of healing. And that is why I called my introduction "Prelude." This is the beginning of my heart's song.

I look back and I'm thankful for the heart-wrenching, emotional abuse I experienced over the course of 2019. It's so strange how we are born into a world that is so unforgiving about what it takes away. Or, how we are born with the ability to love someone with all our being, despite how wrong a match they are for us.

I've learned that love is completely blind. And if your eyes can still see through the blinding red, love is committed, scared, and ignorant all at once. Love is powerful enough to make you step beside yourself and let little pieces of your heart die as they make room for the problems of someone else. But love is also kind. It's peaceful and unbelievably pleasant. The language of new and unscathed love calls with a force so powerful that forgotten pieces of your soul find their way home after they have drifted off into almost non-existence. I've learned after spending so much time diving into the dark that love has a way of bringing your soul back to life, even after being the reason for tearing you apart. That's what these poems are: the redemption of my heart and soul.

~ ~ ~

Before I climbed out of the emotionally draining hole I dug myself into, I pictured myself as such a fragile mess of feelings. It felt surprisingly good to dive into the painful embrace of the past. It allowed me to feel *something*, even if all I could feel was pain from my memories. I found that forcing myself to sit in silence created the perfect place for my pain to fester, for my heart to hurt instead of beat lifelessly in a loud world that distracted me. I wandered through my mind and found happy memories, but I could no longer relate to them. The people I spoke to each day could barely connect with me. When reaching out to the closest people in my life, their advice, compliments, and whole-heartedness hardly cracked the layers of ice forming around me. Then, I found something I needed to put me on a path of healing. I found my tree.

I walked past my tree many times without acknowledging it. When I finally took note of my tree, I froze. I had never seen a tree shedding its bark in such a fantastic way. I witnessed the bark of this eucalyptus tree hang on nothing, as if floating just above the surface. The bark seemed to be frozen in place, taking on the appearance of suspended ribbons sprouting from a bow on a bouquet of flowers. This tree held up eighty feet of wood with roots that tore into the earth without restraint. It was immaculate.

I walked by my tree every day for months and would just stop to stare at it. The world threw strong winds that tested the tree's foundations, dry heat that baked its leaves and branches, and lowly bugs that lived on and burrowed into the trunk. It seemed like I would notice something new it had to deal with every time I passed by. Then came the day when the bark finally fell off. It had me initially upset, but that same day echoed to me how the tree was ready to reveal its smooth ivory trunk. Despite everything, the tree had grown.

I was effortlessly drawn to its unique, ribbon-like bark, the piercing shades of white that broke through the cracks, and the unhindered base of roots that kept the tree upright and strong. It felt like God was whispering to me through the rustling of leaves and the reflections of light bouncing off the pristine surface. This eucalyptus tree was the inspiration I didn't know I needed to give a foundation to my work. It helped drive me in a direction of growth instead of simply using my words to express pain.

~ ~ ~

I have to warn you, *Tree Bark* is heavy. "Ravaged Roots" begins and ends in a state of complete devastation and each poem holds a piece of a broken soul. The poems evolve in "Burrowing Beetles" to show heartbreak and betrayal from various stages and show how those moments played into my journey. They grow to become contemplative in "Falling Leaves" and talk about how my thoughts festered as my emotions started to explore a strange form of healing. In

"Silent Ascent," the poems traverse reminiscent feelings of pain just before rising into a state of acceptance. The final part, "Aubade," is an utterly blissful dedication to the woman I love and explains just how happy I have become after finally learning to grow, too.

This is a collection of my deepest sorrows and my highest triumphs. These poems are my thoughts. They are my desires. They are my questions. They are my wonders. They are my mind divided into its most vulnerable parts. They represent the path I have taken to recover my heart and soul. I am honored that you are reading my work. I hope the path I have carved into the fine grains of poetry is deep enough for your roots to take form and grow as mine have.

Don't forget, we are always growing.

Stay rooted,
Lance

Part I

Ravaged Roots

Air in My Hand

They tell me hello and say goodbye without
knowing how frantically my heart is crying.

I never mean for my smile to tell them lies,
but the chasing numbness never subsides.

I yearn for the tides of my mind to find peace
from my recent demise. I am just a man, who is

lost and in decline, taking my place among
those who replaced the air in their hands

with the hands of their lover. I watch the rest
of the world, the way they hold on to each other.

I pass them by, and I crack inside. I see the
others beaming and alive and I find myself

nearby, acting like I am part of it all, while
trying to forget that my soul has died.

Burned Bridges

There was an ample burning in the bones
of my chest setting each breath I took into
unrest. My empty stomach was pressed by
an encumbering air that formed trench-widened
eyes; I could only stare. The anxiety became

        too dense, too heavy, too intense

and it plummeted below without recompense.
My chest fell empty and my belly overflowed
with the eroded remains of my tongue.
The fragments of my
decaying lungs clung to
my stomach's walls
lined with

        green, how undeniably
        sickening. Bitter
        anxieties fell into the
        spaces between.
        That's what I get
        for letting
        my bridges
        burn away.

Now, I'll stare across
this ripped open crevice
contemplating the
decisions I have made.

That Night

I remember when it happened.
I was walking a straight line,
minding my tongue,
but speaking my mind,
and I tripped—knocked my head—
on something tiny and small.
I guess I took it with me
to bed that night in the
cold of the lengthy fall.
It was harmless
                              at first.
It grew strong and tall.
The thirst it gave me was
so intense I had to crawl.
It became my new desire.
I didn't mind my shortfall.

It set my bridges on fire—
it didn't matter how appalled
I felt. I kept chasing as it burned
and ravaged my skin.
I was enthralled.

But the realization of the hurting
instilled a new reason to try and recall—

fall up into the light,
escape the burning,
escape the hunger,
the famished churning,
the curious drive,
the vengeful yearning.

It called the cuts in my skin
affection. I tried to let go of
the fire and shuffle in a new
direction, but it held on with
its infectious barbs and wires.

I winced when it carved into my
nerve endings and melted away the
comfort of the known. I was forced
to let pain guide me to promised
mending, and it continued to bite
worse whenever I tried to let go.

Matthew

I'm not sure if you were always here or
if you just decided to appear that night,
but I don't like you. Everything about you
is chaos ensuing, but for you to choose
blundering idiocy and hideous scenes
is not beyond you, apparently.

When I stop and think I have relief
from all the demons chasing me,
you choke my soul so I can't breathe.
I'm cursed to run and clench my teeth,
find a place to hide and weep.

I need you to see the path you
have me walk leaves me no
place to grieve.

Devil's Laugh

I made an unusual choice, just yesterday,
and felt myself, again, turn from my good ways.
I gambled once more for the sake of adrenaline
and felt my soul tear and wear its regrets.

As I knelt, alone, on my bedroom floor,
mere inches away from my mirrored closet door,
I stared into my brown eyes, full of confusion,
wondering why I gave in to selfish delusions.

I curled up in a ball and I quietly asked
Why are you doing this? When will I be free?
The devil laughed as I laid back crying. He said
You did this to yourself. You belong to me.

Black River

I wake each day to fight for the light
withheld by a river of black that lingers
and flows. I resist the dark that sputters
and grows, but simple pleasures sit just
below. I should have worked harder to
stop myself, and I tried, but I am just stuck,
I suppose. I dove in and sank to the bottom.
I want to know where that hidden light goes;
it's like it shows for anyone but myself. But I

stay in this endless river of addiction,
this place of addled desires and hopes,
heartlessly cradled by ashen snow.

The Hatch

opened slowly as his hunger was fed.
The boy he was is surely dead after all
those nights lying awake in bed, heart
pounding 'til his face turned red.

When the hatch opened full swing,
it spewed out dark things. The boy
grew older, turned himself into a
fling multiple times a week.

He stayed awake at night, avoiding sleep,
trapped in a room that watched him weep.
He stayed in that bed as it continued to reap
his poor little mind, that has-been king.

He slipped away from firmer ground,
slipped away from his golden crown.
The dark from the hatch dragged him down
and the monster within dragged him around.

He wept each night for a place to rest his mind,
laid in the shadows to escape the monster's bite.
His body suffocated without the light, and he cried
with the rending desire for the darkness to die.

Mirror Man

The empathetic peering of those oaky eyes complemented the respect I had for him. He used to tell me about how endlessly the world would turn as I walked about it restlessly. His eyes were filled with a strange longing for the adventure paved by the sun's dawning.

I don't see him anymore.
He deserted me.
He went out the door.

I searched for his infectious smile in the reflection, and I only found a frown that spoke of his rejection. I do not think my persistence was enough to convince him to come back. He is avoiding me, keeping his distance, folding closed his heavy eyelids in light of my decisions.

I miss him—he made me alive and complete.
I miss the sepia brown that was so easy to see.
I miss the lack of flared nostrils whenever we would meet. My arrogance made his abrupt retreat a choice not taken as rude in the least.

I know he is somewhere, tucked away,
hiding from the monster inside my brain.
I don't believe he'll return to my side during
my numbing days or barbed wire nights.

I have to try and forget him for the rest
of my life, live on despite the darkness
in my mind. Maybe if I keep trying, it
won't be pain that remains. Maybe
he'll come back, and

I won't be so afraid.

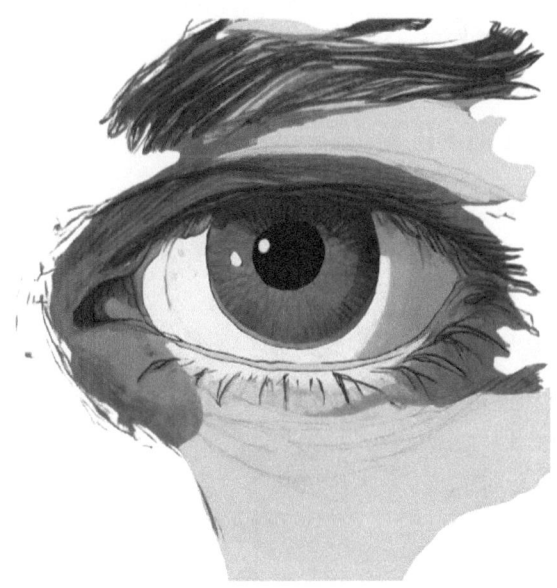

Bricks on Top

block out the light,
the calming rain.
I sit in my quiet room,
hiding in the shade,
yearning for life to return
to my soul one day.

I'm nowhere near the sun,
I've built deep underground.
I'm scared to reach out because
the dark might pull me down.

I parted from the sky,
built down past the hills,
to get away from the lies,
the chaos the world instills.

I would rather stay under,
brokenhearted until the
ground stops being filled
with days of stunted time,
the loss of my iron will.

trickling

sit and stare
only alone
no body there
no way to atone
hate being grown
lost track of my soul
miss being little

does life have a goal
must i be so brittle
borderline boredom
life's greatest zero sum
no music
no desire to hum
do the clouds stay apart
always a lack of answers

emptiness filling my heart
head rolling and heavier eyelids
betting on others is the worst bid
i've known sadness since i was young
silence creeps closer from shadows behind
the walls of white are my warden tonight
even my reflection has lost sight of me

contemplation never feigns a grasp on my time
jealousy and captivity are making me blind
i forgot where my demons hide
is that the sun setting or rising outside
the world i live in is making my head a mess
forget the time when time was slow
grab onto time's waist and let the hurt go

    empty and vacant and desperate and
    angry and caring and intemperate and
    alone and numb and so delicate

i just need that love again
i will not pretend to know
love didn't have to end
in the end i tend to sit quietly
but no one will see
or even understand

the guilt and loneliness will remain
on two broken legs will i never stand
now i just stare at the ceiling
invite sleep to take the feeling
wake up and forget the reeling

another day added to my bucket

Part II

Burrowing Beetles

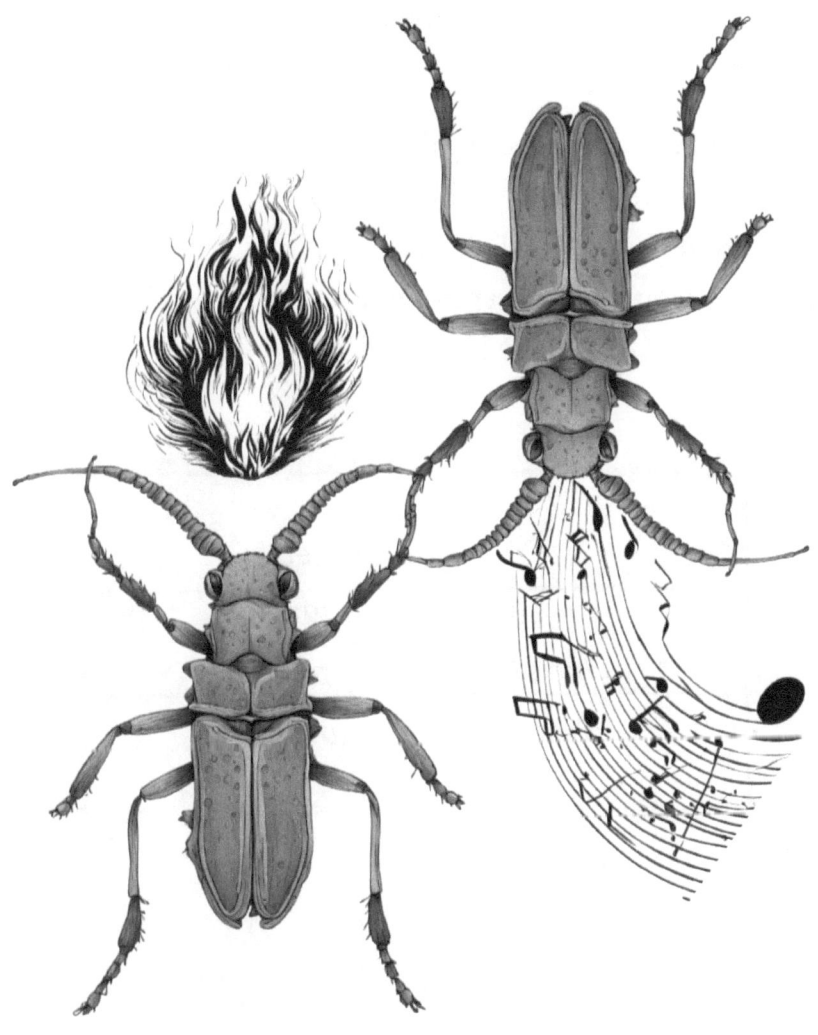

Lemonade Stand

I carefully crafted and nailed
together a wooden table. I created
an attractive label that said

Mine is Better

and waited for the never-ending
lines to appear. I sat excitedly and
perfectly still with pristine pitchers
of lemonade, but nobody came to
my stand.

On one of my unsuspecting days,
a queen walked past my table, her
heart in her hand, and I did what
any man would to get her to swing
back his way. I fashioned a little
wooden sign to say:

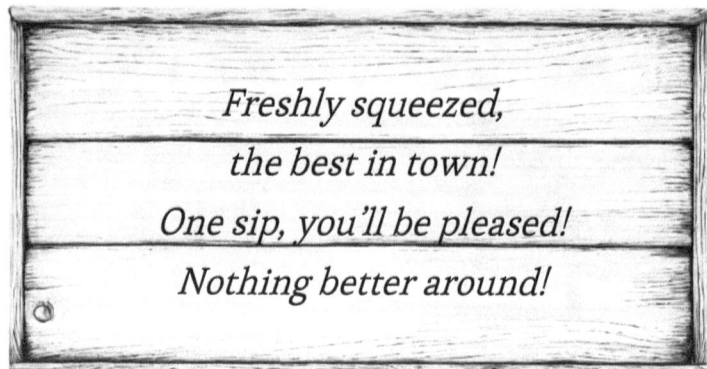

*Freshly squeezed,
the best in town!
One sip, you'll be pleased!
Nothing better around!*

She took a sip and found herself drinking
more each day. She would drink every
pitcher I made, but suddenly started
throwing them, empty, at the ground.
I cobbled together a new sign that read:

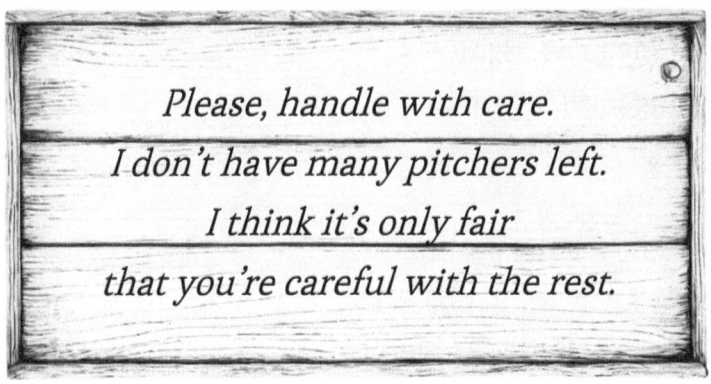

*Please, handle with care.
I don't have many pitchers left.
I think it's only fair
that you're careful with the rest.*

Those finicky wooden signs
helped me find her finely kept
heart firmly planted in my hands,
but she held the glasses from my
lemonade stand much less carefully
than I thought she would.

I refused to give her more
when she begged for another
sip. I had no more to give.

I sent her away, and I stayed
behind to pick up the glass
she left with me that day.
While wiping my tears
and cleaning her mess,
I realized I had no more
pitchers left. I held the
glass in my hand, tightly
squeezing until it gashed
and bled.

These scars are my reminder
of where my heart has been led.
These scars help me to mind her
when her memories flood my head.

The Queen's Burning Tongue

Her lips and her tongue
spit young sounds of fire
that rang aloud. Liquid
apathy poured down
and puddled as she
melted my crown.

Although entrusted to uphold her
king's palace, her words were sewn
with baffling malice. They felt so much
worse because they came from her.
My ears callus from the noise, my
eardrums ruptured and destroyed.

Our tomorrow
was supposed to allow
the sorrow to subside—
let the pieces billow

up into the sky, up
       into the light, high
              with the winds
          as the sun grew dim.

Talking to each other was supposed
to help love survive and make the
long wait of time seem more like a
walk and less like a climb.

Instead, engravings of her angry
voice were burned into my soul and
were never seen by other's eyes,
never seen by family at home. Her
words painted over and stabbed
what beauty I had and opened the
door for a creature who wanted to
ruin me. In the dark, it set me on
fire after splashing me in oil.
The flames bubbled my flesh,

      made it boil,
           made it shrink
                and rip
           and coil.

I became a scattered dust
as her words stopped molding.
The controlling conjecture captured
the breathlessness of my soul when
her words stopped reciting their love
to uphold collapsing holes.

The Quiet of the White Car

It wasn't the melted crown that left me
with scars, that forced the trembling
upon my lip. It was the crawling dead
silence, the quiet of the white car.

Those teary eyes and dropped jaw
had nothing to say when I turned the
car off that day. I sat awkwardly in my
dying-white car, parked by a curb under
barely visible stars. The ringing in my
ears made me believe the ongoing
silence would offer no relief.

It was an overbearing quiet,
taller than giant beanstalk giants,
holding steady in firm defiance.
I asked her to speak, and her eyes
became inflamed. I found her silence
forcing itself upon me, forcing my
mind into untamable submission.

Lost in my feelings, I started reeling, peeling through my thoughts. I tried reaching out despite silence's rotted ringing tearing us in two. I lost time over who was blaming who, and who was at fault for dropping the ball. A fruitless call for hurt to leave.

That seething silence that pierced me, regardless of who is around, somehow remains embedded, still remains so loud. Still in my mind, still in my memories, keeping me stuck in my fretful doubts. Never letting the screams from underneath breach the veil of silence none can perceive.

It wasn't the melted crown that left me with scars, that forced the trembling upon my lip. It was the crawling dead silence, the quiet of the white car.

The Fire That Finally Faded Away

The dark moved quietly
through my mind while
you made my heart the
home of our love in decline.

Bearing the fire from your lips,
the abuse from your power trips,
and the sharpness of your eyes
led my life to unsubtle demise.

The demons I had to face,
that you so lovingly helped
sew to my soul, haunt me
during the days and nights
I am alone.

The yelling that melted my crown,
the conjecture, and the lack of sound
formed ice inside when your fire
was no longer around to burn me.

The Fire That Had Burned Me

I used to hate that fifth day of April.
I was held back by heartache's pull.

I didn't understand how to let go.
I thought that day ruined my hold

on my heart, my mind, my will to be bold.
I was definitely wrong, there is no doubt.

And it was a beautiful song, but it wasn't that
loud. It was in the final months I finally learned

not to stay and keep getting burned. I chose
to keep my heart happy and walked away.

But my attempts to leave were made in vain.
The fires I tried so desperately to escape

left scars on my heart that glistened with shame.
No matter what road I paved, it all felt the same;

no matter what I distracted myself with, the cold came.
That is, until I took a chance on warming my hands

on the very same fire that branded me. I was
stuck in the snow, where my heart was stranded.

I was desperate for warmth in the darkness. I could
not get away from the loneliness I was handed.

I was scared it would, again, bubble and boil my flesh,
but it was nothing but a comfort, I must confess.

Though her fire scarred me for the rest of my days,
after all the time I spent baked in a waltzing pain,

I am still undoubtedly and wholeheartedly amazed
at the ways she caused me to grow and change.

Crimson Lake

Transparent meteors endlessly fell
down the windowpane as the tears
on my face did the same. I grew
colder than could be explained. A
fortress of ice formed and did not
fail to contain the warmth once
held by my empty heart.

No past, no present, no future, no time.
There was no blood flowing in this red lake
of mine. There was no longer an ebb
pushing life through the caves. The blood
stopped moving when my heart found its grave.

No strength could reach the icy center.
The frozen layers were too deep. That is,
until the sun rose again on the eighth day
and presented a creation God had made. A
vessel of gold, cobalt-blue windows to the
soul, and riches untold by a love unknown.

Her presence warmed the frozen surface.
She tried to thaw the ice with unusual purpose.
But the veins of red that had been frozen for so long
would not thaw when she sang her song.

Between Her Fingers

I thought it was over,
the way my mind dove
into the abyss, hoping to
find bliss in the darkness.
I still dive in, and I'm flooded
with fright, onyx shadows
crossing my eyes.

Why did you take it from me,
my ability to love and breathe?
I hate that I don't hate you.
I hate that I feel so numb.

Pretending you were the one broke
me into the pieces of a person I can't
see in the mirror. I could feel nothing
when her fingers fell between my
fingers. And I wanted to love her, or
anyone, but the ashes from your fire
haven't settled.

The Fire That Was Never There

I was too scared to ever be burned again

        and then

that cobalt-blue windowed vessel of gold
took hold of the convalescent cracks
wrapped around my heart.

She showered me in affection before she
stopped holding on to her old, chopped love.
My heart was still getting rid of those slowly
fading sutures I had placed upon it the year
before. I don't know who wanted it more,
but neither of us were ready.

Still swarming with the ceaseless dust,
I gave in to my lust, and I must not lie,
I felt guilty for lying down with her at night.
Our licentious love was never overcome
by the drumming of foul play. I was dumb
for allowing each passing day to be filled
with passive affection and repressive decay.

The Fire She Thought We Had

I could only capture her fire with the
little matchstick between my fingertips
since I no longer had a candlewick.
The oncoming brokenhearted hardships
bombarded our sense of delight.
Even though I kept her fire safe and nearby,
my used up, wickless candle could not light.

I thought, deep inside, that I could hide
my hurting heart given enough time.
But I lied when I convinced myself
that my love for her was not in decline.
She never made herself out to be a whore,
but she had preyed upon another man
when she opened her locked doors to
steal his love on thin, jealous lines.

Her warmth between my fingers started
to fade, so, like the last fire, I let go. Her
teary eyes may have paved the way for
me to contemplate the choice I made, but I
know better than anyone, sometimes you
have to pinch that burning flame
so you can learn to be okay.

Leo and Libra

The first was conceited. Always heated,
a Leo full of bravado. She stole the key
to my heart. The worst part, she is so far
from me now, but I still remember the
sounds flying from her mouth, screaming
loud, holding my soul down.

I remember

I was scolded for sighing at the sound
of sweet nothings whispered in my ear
from she who had just hurt me. I was
scolded on Cypress Drive, pressed by
impressively loud lungs for wanting
to go out to lunch. I was scolded by a
self-centered fire, a line of confusion
that seemed to capsize the emotional
coming of the sunrise. I was crying out
for losing time, flying away from pain
and blame and shame and training
myself to smile when I was in denial
or compiling my mind.

Then there was the second: the little Libra.
Labeled as another lasting love.
Lying next to me, lying to me,
lying with other men.

Going on adventures that ended
with pathetic explanations for her
absence. I couldn't pretend her sense
of desire in other men wasn't her rule
of thumb. After all, that was how I
earned her love.

I should have known to leave her alone
when she hid the texts while I was home
or changed the names in her phone.
I should have known, too well,
what befell a heart prone to pattern,
the feelings earned by a person packing
their love into more than one heart.
I should have known we would fall
apart when another man gave her a
lower bar that was too easy to grasp.
There I was, pretending it all would last,
like the actions of the past didn't matter.

Was it love? Obligation?
Looking back, it was always the latter.

Part III

Falling Leaves

Sway

When a loved one passes away, it changes the
world as you know it. Your way of life becomes
erratic and broken, but

                you take their loss with a token of faith.
                    Maybe you hope, maybe you pray,
                      they have found a happier place.

You have to stay behind, in wake of your sadness.
It's difficult to find light in a world so unforgiving
and unkind. But, then you'll hear people say

                "Time will provide you with a space away
                  from pain. It will come when you're
                  patient and have learned to keep your
                    hurt restrained." You have to

learn to be complacent when you feel the
sway between feeling broken and

                        feeling okay.

The Blue Balloon

It's trapped up there in the dark,
near the walls and the tall ceiling,
away from anyone's reach,
away from anyone's healing.

It's having trouble falling down below.
It sways back and forth on a metal pipe.
It can't return from the lonely shadows.
It's stuck up there, hidden from the light.

It got stuck because it was let go.
It fell away from hands that used to hold
on tight and keep it from feeling alone.
It's lonelier than anybody will ever know.

Battle with Exhaustion

I can feel the window's blind
weight creeping shut over
my bloodshot sight. My day is
exhaustion's to reap because I
failed to meet with sleep. Baggy
are the saggy windows straining
in front of my brain. My back aches
as my hand trembles. I cannot tell
what the distance resembles.

My head tilts.
My body leans.
I try to understand
what words mean.
With no regard for me,
exhaustion takes charge.
My movements slop,
my thoughts drop
out of my mind.
My head is topless.
The mess of dreams
pour out and line the sheets
of paper covered in scribbled
exchanges of words.

It is strange.

A truce with my sleepy alter ego
and the constant grasp of exhaustion's hold
is making the world feel a little less cold.

Chained in a Dream

My mind fell into the dark,
bound tightly in its shackles.

A dream was born
and I listened to it babble.

I fell into chilling waters
and listened to my chains rattle.

My dream whispered,
"Relax, you're still alive."

"I'm going to die and I'm not even twenty-five!"
I gasped for air and cried.

A familiar face sauntered closer and asked,
"Why are you struggling? Nobody is around."

I seethed in panic, searching for help nearby.
"Take me back! Get me out! I've almost drowned!"

It contemplated my answer and replied,
"But, look where you are. What do you see?"

I looked around and saw my tree.
I finally caught enough air to respond.

I wiped my tears and asked,

"How can I feel like I'm drowning
in such a little pond?"

When I Cry

The world tells me
I can kill a person
with my bare hands,
that I have the strength
to be the last man standing.

The world tells me to embrace
a more tender side of myself,
to handle each moment with
discretion, a fistful of repression.

The world asks me
why I'm not supportive
of everyone else's fears,
the problems of society,
the issues that plague our
world with endless anxiety.

*You don't cry enough. Open up
and listen to our problems blossom into
a flurry of tears. Our problems aren't
mere simple fixes, listen well and
don't dismiss us.*

So, I put aside my life
and time, even when
I'm not fine, to help
with their whining.

                I try crying.

Then, the world tells me
I am being too emotional.
They say bottle it up,
keep it to myself and
quit crying.

You cry too much.
Stop coming to us with your
problems and your fears. No,
we don't want to hear about
your problems, we can't stand them.
Grow up. Be a man.

My problems are like poison
to their hypocritical ears.
I have to stay quiet when my
patience is in decline. Funnel
my anger into my mind, not
into my fists.

Paint a picture that lifts the
mood of the room with words
that tunnel away from my sad
heart's tune.

Let the boiling blood drift off.
Less rage, more calm.
Less anger, more tender palms.

I have to battle with patient
restraint to avoid any escalation
because encounters with louder tones
are so drastically frowned upon.

Come on
Crisis
Subtle
Internalized
Uproar

I have to try and live my life hiding behind
my quiet lies to stop them from seeing me

when I cry.

Heartache's Blade

Your heart is always yours, do not let this fact
be mistaken. You entrust it to someone who
leaves your soul shaking. The body finds itself
overwhelmed and quaking with the slightest
touch of a love that's overtaking.

>A love that promises to never fall away.
>A love that promises to stay the same.

However, there is a truth we leave alone and
unspoken, because it closes the mind and leaves
the soul choking. The truth can lie in the promise
that was made if the promise is lost and the heart
is betrayed.

>Just because two hearts found a way,
>it doesn't mean they have found their place.

You need to be careful when you decide to say
you will love them always and every single day.
Your heart and your soul will be so afraid if
heartache decides to brandish its blade.

Searching for Love

It's funny.

I find myself wanting to play,
from time to time, these days.
Play the game that ruined me,
that sent my heart into decay.

I want to play,
aimlessly, shamefully, insatiably.
Wait for the emotion in my heart
to take. Feel time fly when I chase
after love online. Feel my mind
crash like water on the coastline.

I'd only play a little.
It's fine if I play.
Even if I start to lose.
It's going to be okay.

No, no. I hate it.
The days to weeks,
the months to years,
wasting my energy,
waiting for new love
to appear. I fear I will
never find it again.

Temporary

An inward folding of sacred moldings carves
into colder parts of my old self. The incessant
leviathans from an endless ocean swim out
and run at the falling sun. Shadows sew
doubt that light exists in a bout of loud
and radical clouds. The further inside the
darkness hides, the more I am shown how

I am rotting. I am alone.

Teeth grind below my mind. Hordes of pain
form within my jawline. Clenched hands
cover clenched eyes and hold back the tides
as they try to rise against frightful hardships.
God will eventually come and help me take flight,
but the right to life, in spite of time, only feels
sublime when I feel fine. The walls of kindness
I lie behind only bind light to my soul for so long.
These excruciating fake smiles only settle my
mind for mere moments. My need for noise
suppresses the unending lack of wholeness.

They see me smile and let me fake and pretend,
and I pretend all I can while I wait for loneliness
to end. Strange, so strange, the danger that rages
on under waves of passion that come and go.

In one moment, I'm in control, and then I'm tossed
into the familiar moments of a hard place and stone.

Don't go, don't go. Please don't go.

I'm tired of losing what I know to cancer's hold.
It seems like taking the ones I love never gets old.
How can I continue down this road? The end isn't
here and I'm not even close, but the world doesn't
care, and it always shows. I'm expected to explain
that I'm not in pain. The sun sits while the moon
visits. The storm closes in.

Rain.

Showers from a finite source within shake
out and trample my will to stay awake
as the crimson water of the frozen lake
starts to freeze over again.

Am I sane? Is something wrong with my brain?
Does what I say not come off the page as a rage-
induced call for what little parts of me remain?
The constant temptation of a tasteful future
full of tireless promises and tangy love
floods an ominous sense of violent isolation.

It never lasts, and it never stays.
Time always scoffs after keeping
happiness from me because it knows
I have no say over its ways. And I
am so tired of feeling this pain, but
I know this feeling will end

    someday.

Listen to Your Sad Songs

The sad songs you play, day after day,
night after night, work to heal your mind.
When you let a person step inside your
frightful sadness, they will find

the sad songs you listen to
aren't how you should thrive.
They'll say you're biding time,
not facing your heart's decline.

> *Just listen to happy songs.*
> *The sad songs are so wrong.*
> *How long until you smile?*
> *How long is "in a while?"*
> *How much longer do you*
> *need them? How long?*

That is when I say,

As long as it takes
to stop the aches.

As long as it takes
to cure the heartbreak.

Never Mind

I'm fine.

My mind is better,
        no more cracks.

Never mind. The memories.
        They are coming back.
                Oh, the memories I've had.

Never mind.
        The memories have been taken.

Never mind.
        They are in my crypt. I was mistaken.

My dreams. They knew I was a liar.
        My dreams show only one desire.
                But never mind that either.

Oh, that was quick.
        It was just my mind, again.
                Playing tricks.

I'm glad it wasn't something I missed.

No, no. Never mind.

I miss it every day.
      I don't want to stay away.
            My mind is not mine.

Never mine.
Never my mind.
My mind is not mine.
My mind is never mine.
Never mind what isn't mine.

Oh, never mind.

            I'm fine.

Part IV

Silent Ascent

Until the Wind Comes

I have been told that flowers dance in the wind.
I believe the wind dances in the flowers.

Their petals, their stems, their roots in the ground,
all slow to move, until the wind comes around.

Flowers grow freely and reach for the sky,
but never dance until the wind passes by.

The Wind's Promise

As the dust started to settle
from my crumbling heart,
the wind came and visited me
with the promise of a new start.
The wind would take away the pain
and help toss the aching aside.
The wind's promise would be made
if I promised to let my hurt die.

I felt the wind leave my fingertips
and it took the promise away with it.
It assured me it would return when I
asked for a visit. But before it was gone,
it had one final request.

Call to me when you're ready.
Only then and nothing less.
Call to me when you're steady,
when your heart finally finds rest.

Over My Shoulder

In a different city,
near my old job,

I made memories in a two-story apartment,
built for two and taken over by four.
It was there I watched a cheater
splatter a friend's heart all over the floor.

Just down the street,
less than a mile away,

I made memories in a dingy house
built for five and taken over by six.
It was there I watched toxic people live
dully with their stones and sticks.

Up the freeway,
near a dirt trail,

I made memories in a boonies duplex,
cheaply built for one and rented by two.
It was there I watched an ex decide to
pick and choose like I wasn't hers to lose.

I would pass these places,
on my way to work,
and remember the ways my life went berserk.
Gosh, did it hurt to remember the eyes of
a betrayed friend welling up in disbelief
as her world came to an end.

It hurt to remember the
screams from late at night

breaking through thin walls, landing on ears
barely lit with moonlight. It hurt to
remember a person who said they loved
me fall prey to the cliché of jealousy's weight.

And then, on no different
or special day,

I came near one of my old homes, the
dingy house just off the road. The same
home whose walls condoned bad habits
and suspicions blown out of proportion.

I soon realized I drove
past that old home,

that dingy two-story I used to roam, and
I was wide-eyed, even surprised, to think

I passed by and didn't cry a little inside.
In that moment, enough time had finally
passed without me being reminded of the
people I left behind. I could go anywhere,
and pay no mind to the broken memories
over my shoulder. I could go anywhere, and
know the pain was finally over.

Sanguine Letters

I was hurting more than I could say.
I felt there would eventually come a
day when the life we wanted would
slip away. How do you tell somebody,
who gave you all their love,

"I need to let go. I need to be okay."

The letter I wrote was sent with
dismay. It spoke my words for me,
woven in pain. It told my old flame
I could not stay with her any longer.
That letter was never real, only pixels
and bytes. I sent it hoping it would
make things right. But, sending it left
a sour taste on my tongue because I
wasn't sure if she was the one.

The response I got froze and burned me,
and I finally knew we weren't on the same
journey. I could have sent a handwritten
letter like I used to. Fill it with heart
and some jokes, too. Carefully wrap it in
red and seal it in love. Mention, in some
fashion, the God up above.

I have so many hidden letters left
in my head because some things are
better left unsaid. Even though the
words will never be written, my heart
is beating and no longer frostbitten.

I think I'll write more letters to others.
Some for my friends, some for their mothers.
Some for strangers, even some for my brothers.
These will be different from that one before.

They won't tear down a soul at its burning core,
won't stop a person from seeing me anymore,
won't cause love to become cold and sore,
won't destroy what two people hoped for,
won't leave a bleeding heart on the floor,
won't create solemn and emotional gore.

No more, no more! I say no more!
These letters will differ from that
one before. Love and love only—
nothing more.

Heart in Hand

I look back in time and see myself holding
my heart by my side and someone else's
heart in my hand. I see others standing in
line just waiting for me to hold theirs, too.

That's what I used to do. I pushed aside my
life and all my failings to make room for
their stories, their hurting, and their
wailing. I carried the weight of their words.

I heard about the weight of the world being
too much for their tired soul to endure. I sat
through each story, tried to reassure them that
they were acting silly, naive, and immature.

But, it's true.

The problems of others had an allure, an
unavoidable attraction my mercy devoured.
I was dedicated to every person. I listened for
hours and felt myself worsen. I listened with
a tongue tied, like my own thoughts weren't
hiding behind my eyes. I never spoke out
against any who shouted for my help.

I let their problems overshadow my own
and pretended to atone for my mistakes by
helping others with theirs. I couldn't help
but hold them close and create a haven of
safety for those still hanging on. It felt like
a curse I had to bear because I would have
rather overdosed on the hope of others
than sit with my problems alone. I think
I have held in my hand the heart of each
person I know. I would have rather let
myself go than see the people I love
go away.

After all this time, though, I finally know
what people mean when they say,

"Love yourself, first."

It isn't about others who wait in line. It's
about realizing I am not cursed to uphold
other people's lives. I'll always do my best
to remain kind, but I have learned to
distinguish between the lines others stand in
and the line drawn within my mind. And now,
more than ever before, I will keep riding
along in this fine life without the worry
of leaving myself behind.

Without the TV On

When it was time for sleep, I could feel the past pouring
from my head. I laid there squirming, alone and upset,
while painful thoughts fell onto my bed. Each night, I

asked the broad and black-rimmed rectangle of light
to speak to me, stop the room from feeling so quiet.
The sound spoke over the riots that raged on from past

years and hushed her screaming memory within my
mind's ear. A night came where the TV only seemed to
anger me with its screeching, so I turned it off.

I waited for the unceasing sound of the scolding voice to
return. I clenched my eyes, clenched my jaw, and waited
for the mental mauling to freeze and burn. In my mind,

I found there was no sound to be heard. Not a single
thought stirred. I laid in that bed thankful the memories
were gone. Every night since,

I've slept without the TV on.

The Quiet of the Night

I could never hear their light.
I could only stare up at the
blackness salted with serenity.

Faded in my wake, berated by
my own thoughts, I watched
while stars paraded and sang
distant songs with cadences
too stellar to contain in my
little brain. The flashing
whites passed in the silent
sky with everlasting flickers
as I fell into the short buzz
of a few shots of liquor.

Those distant embers stunting my
rage and dawdling temper have
swept across the sky each night
giving the world their splendor.

It was quiet.

It was so quiet.

How they burn, how they burn,
all through the night, despite
being held behind the moon's
silver limelight.

It wasn't until they arrived
without songs of her quiet spite
that I realized these stars,
as they paraded the sky,
were the quiet I needed
all this time.

The Sun's Kisses

She arrives every day and then runs off to hide,
leaving us alone to fend for warmth and light.
And yet, despite her daily departing, it is her
warm delight that brings us back from the
coldest nights.

True, when she kisses our skin, our pores scream,
forcing our bodies to bleed water. We also find staring
directly at her is extremely unwise because she
brandishes her teeth and sinks them into our eyes.
And, if we choose to turn and run away, we can feel her
kisses chasing close behind, waiting for a chance to
wrap around our fragile spines.

Though she may kiss us a little harder than we desire,
she works hard to mend and heal us with soothing
fire. She isn't kissing us with a thousand teeth that
tear our bodies asunder. She is giving us a thousand
kisses that fill our souls with wonder.

The next time you are given thunder and rain,
remember she is somewhere above the storm,
patiently waiting to kiss away the pain.

I Skip the Sad Songs

They were my anthem. A habit formed from a handsome amount of abuse. They were the drug I used to solder my mind with less ugly muses of the past. They would play in each passing second, and I found comfort in the frown that formed.

A journey through life later and time's infinite blade had cut away the pain from each waking moment. No longer did the sad songs play when I found myself alone at home, in my car on the road, or bored on my phone. I didn't begin each day with a playlist made to tame raging blue flames. That isn't to say I stopped enjoying the sad songs. They were the catalyst for something

                      beautiful.

But I have tried to play my old heart-remedies, and the weight they carry is no longer something I wish to feel on my shoulders. I understand that my grief has been put to rest. No more testing my resolve with problems unsolved. Those wishes to live with my heartache are finally gone because whenever I hear music, I skip the sad songs.

Bumble Bee

Sweet little bumble bee,
with your eyes of emerald green,
please keep singing your song for me.

Because of you, I am finally free,
floating along happily. You flew
in from a distant Apple Valley,
from your distinct little hive,
to show me the beauty
and light in my life.

I am flowing with the wind
beside your wings and the
future feels so promising.
The flowers are dancing
and the sun shines bright.
I can borrow your stability
when I struggle with mine.
You found a way to climb
inside and warm the cold
parts of my mind. I am so
happy with the smile you
provide. You help me forget
my heart had died.

When I'm lying awake,
thinking of you each night,
I thank God for gifting me
a light to call mine.

Part V

Aubade

Eucalyptus Rubida

That old bark held on,
sorrowful and frustrated,

unprepared for the growth
that waited to push out

and overcome the
lingering hatred.

The old bark of the tattered
eucalyptus tree fell away and

no longer hangs with an essence
of misery. Time brushed against

the old and dry surface to help
the new skin grow and thrive.

The precious pristine,
hidden and discrete,

clawed and elbowed a
way out to breathe.

Immaculate ivory was
irreversibly revealed

by the smooth trunk
that was once concealed.

The tree will always encounter
another year of change and

a new ring will form
to welcome the new day.

Between Two Pine Trees

I walked out of the house
completely unsure of where
I'd go. I knew I wanted to go
somewhere out of town.
Somewhere I could smile,
where time might slow down.

I candidly crossed off places I
had been. After some thought,
I remembered a place I wanted
to visit again. It was a rural
mountain town called Oak Glen.

I didn't visit often when I was little and
outspoken, but I remembered it being a
place with rolling hills out in the open.

I thought to myself,

> *if there was going to be a place where time
> could stand still, it would be somewhere
> among those trees that dotted the hills.*

I packed my camera and an extra lens, drove
my car through the mountainous bends. On
my drive, before I arrived, I noticed smaller
trees began to welcome me in. It was like
they had spent their life growing taller to
become my watchful friends.

The sky was mostly cloudy, and a perfect
blue gently reached through the impressive
cold. I could see the trees of old before I turned
the corner into the parking lot. Thankfully,
there were plenty of vacant spots.

I was happy where I parked, near plenty of flowers,
bees, and trees. I looked in a direction and started
walking. I found myself stalking blue birds in the
distance singing songs that were quaint and full
of bliss. I stopped and listened for a while and
found their presence soothing.

When I was young, barely old enough to
speak for myself, I followed these paths
hoping to find something I could adore.
I chose paths I faintly remembered
traveling before, a straight walk this way,
an obtuse left that felt right.

My walk became a hike, with the paved roads
becoming less smooth and more dirt-like.
There was a fork on the path, and I chose the
way less traveled by walking to the right where
the trees effortlessly dazzled. I happened upon
a conservation site, where the path narrowed
with wooden fences. The quiet engulfing me
was tranquil and helped focus my senses:

> I could hear the woodpecker hiding in the tree
> line. His echoes a far cry that complemented the
> buzzing of nearby meadows. I couldn't see him,
> but I saw all the holes he and his brothers built
> over time. I was able to smell the green with all
> the pine wrapping around me.

That was when I came across two trees separated
by just a few feet. They were taller than my neck
felt comfortable stretching back to admire. After
trying to see the peerless spire atop those trees,
I looked down and found a chiseled stone with
a quote. I cleared my throat:

> *Between every two pine trees there*
> *is a door leading to a new way of life.*

I never thought a random fellow named Muir
would help assure me with a quotable cure.
I took a long look at the imaginary door before
me, allowing it to make a lasting impression.
I wondered:

> When I walk through, what will happen?
> My next adventure?
> Maybe I'll find the path to heaven?

Time had stopped. I walked up to the door
and I knocked. After a moment, the door
opened. I walked into my new life.

    And then,
        it began to snow.

When the Snow Falls

Nobody ever told me the
snow sings when it hits
the ground after floating
down in the cold of winter

I felt the slowed *pit* and *pat*
bring me into a blissful daydream.
It was like rain falling in slow motion,
so tenuous and keen on being seen.
It was strange seeing so much green
become plastered in faultless white,
piling high upon the fallen pines.
Then, the snow fell sideways.

The wind came dancing high through
the leaves, rustling them quietly.
My ears faintly rang as chilling flakes
fell into my face and a crease formed.

I smiled.

It had been too long since my defiling numb
was overcome by the sound of silence.
The subtle hum of defiance falling
and biting and climbing on itself

to show my heart to my mind for
the first time since I started the
climb on this journey of mine.

That was when I finally realized
what was hidden from my eyes.

When cold crawls by, I thrive.
When the snow falls, I'm alive.

Peace Among the Leaves

I have found a place in my mind
where everything is quiet for a time.

Where the wind from the seas
comes bathed in subtleties

and I am met with enough relief
to throw me upon my knees.

I feel I can finally breathe.
I bring my mouth to my sleeve

and I cry without clenching my teeth.
My eyes stay open so I can see

all the beauty surrounding me.
It all started with my eucalyptus tree,

and the arrival of bees upon the fallen leaves.
It's a perfect dream carved into the seams,

with the sweet, saintly sap of being free
reminding me of the great man I can be.

The Day You Fell

was when I realized I could die holding your hand
if we were walking along on one of our hikes.

I remember noticing the way the sun was
shining on the fallen pine cones, their dark
brown scales complemented with a golden
tinge of sunlight. We happily explored the
hillside and stepped between hordes of gray
stones and a boundless sea of green trees that
had never known what it was like to be alone.
We heard the birds singing above us with
carefully crafted overtones as the sound
carried itself gently through the forest.

A generous amount of wide-eyed reverence
later, we found an adventurous path held up
by a steep hill of fallen leaves and sticks.

We stood still for just a bit, incautious with
our time, before deciding the best way to
get down the almost-cliff was shuffling
down the side.

I should have gone first because you
slipped and fell. I couldn't tell you how
bad I felt then, but adored you all the
more when you picked yourself up off
the dirt. Little did I know then what
you had in store for me:

more love than I could have ever dreamed of.

The Day a Squirrel Bit You

was the day I fell sweet on your soul.
You, my love, brought snacks to eat.

We sat by the pond, watching a family
near the water, dipping their feet.
From behind a tree came a little squeak,

        a fat squirrel,

poking his head out, wanting a little fruit.
You excitedly offered it green grapes. Sure,

the fat little squirrel was cute, but I
thought it was quite rude when he stuck

his tooth in your fingernail. And that
didn't stop you from trying again.

The Stars are Cold

They exist across all of time and space,
but selfishly keep their warmth hidden
away in a distant, unreachable place.

They are beautiful, though. Swirling
in their unquenchable flames, burning
hotter than you or I will ever know.

So full of raw power, strong enough to
devour anything they touch. But we'll
never get to feel the heat they provide.

To me, the stars are cold.

Even so, it doesn't matter how far away
those stars are. It doesn't stop me from
thinking how I could grow old with you,
enjoying the moments we stare up at the
passing lights in the night sky. Our time
lying here, admiring the hobbling twinkles,
only makes me believe we'll still enjoy the
moments like this when we are old and full
of wrinkles.

They may shine coldly from thousands of
light years away, but while we look up
at the blackened sky and watch as bright
dots saunter by, I feel grounded in our tent,
pitched up poorly in the middle of the desert.

We lie here with nothing but millimeters of
fabric between us and the dirt, looking up
through the netting of see-through holes.
We are seeing double the lights, blurry and
out of focus, because we took the glasses away
from our eyes.

Like looking at the top of a mountain from
miles away, those stars remain beyond reach.
But with you at my side, they could fade away
with their cold light, as carefree and selfishly
as they would like, and they would never burn
or live as long as the love I feel with you tonight.

A New Song

Dots cross the black background
until the closest one of them all
falls up into the sky to light our eyes.
The stars had their silent parade,
and now, a new light shines on the day.
The sky rises with a new dawn,
graciously met by God's embrace.

The birds never seem to sing the
same song they sang a day before.
More of the same sounds, but
played in a different order.

Mortars of light break through
fluffy clouds that still carry the
sound of a quiet night. Dew
drops of ice glow, melting as
the kisses of our home star
break through the crisp,
shivering dark. The world
gives way to nature's hum as
the birds cast a blanket of
sound for the light of the
rising sun.

Home

I closed my eyes.

From outside, I loved the way the sun
bounced off the wide wall of white.
The porch was cradled with warm
wooden fences and a pair of unique
cobblestone pillars in need of
restoration expenses.

I walked through the front door
and the rustic walls were bare. An
open window next to me blew air
into the gossamer curtains.

*This is the place. I've
never been so certain.*

"The home of a commoner," any
other person would say, but I
knew better than any of them what
kind of gem I had on my hands.

I could stand in the middle of the
room and look to the backyard to
see the soon-to-be garden and
miniature farm just next to the
chicken coop we got for a bargain.

I could admire you combing through
our fancy library of old and new books,
feeling astute as you smile at me.

I could smell the freshly grown fruit set
beside the carton of eggs we picked up
from our lovely hens, the aroma of a
healthy breakfast filling the house's den.

I could watch the pictures from our life
tear into barren walls and force them to
wear down the emptiness they once
proudly drowned in.

I could hear the sound of a dog door
flapping open and shut again and again
as our dogs fight over who owns each toy.

I could feel the way our couch lined our
thighs as we watched our favorite movies
to pass the time on a cold summer night.

I opened my eyes.

It may not be real yet, this place we want to own, but someday we'll find it and we'll call it home.

Tree Bark

You've found a way
to push the bark off
on your own.

You've grown.

You've gotten past the
fear of being alone,

or thrown away the hateful
memories you held on to,

or relived the moments of the
past that were hard to go through
without crying yourself to sleep,

or stopped letting people keep you from
helping yourself first because you're
not cursed to uphold their lives,

or taken time to forgive the lies you
were fed when you were vulnerable
and mislead by other's words,

or heard the birds sing a song that did
not distract you for as long as you
could bear without silence ringing
in your head,

or gathered your wits as you lay in bed,
refusing to let the monster drag you
through the red thoughts you always
dreaded,

or, instead of hiding when you started
crying, you cried happy tears when
you told people you loved them,

or survived all of life's mayhem brewing
in the back of your mind as time slowly
forced you to feel like your heart was in
decline,

or climbed out of a hole you dug yourself
into because you thought a lot about how
deep you were going and not how far gone
you were,

or focused on remembering the silent
stars at night instead of her screaming
abuse and the other girl's willingness to
pick and choose like she had nothing to lose,

or refused to lose yourself to past choices
of anguish and pathetic excuses that left
behind a sour taste on your tongue,

or walked among others, old and young,
without being jealous of watching them fill the
air in their hands with whatever they wanted,

or rebuilt the bridges that haunted your
mind and found a way to keep the people
you love bonded to you for life,

or responded to the man in the mirror
with an earful of praise for helping you
find the path back to empathetic ways,

or forgot about the days when you
parked your dying-white car under
the stars that silently tortured your
poor heart and brain,

or changed your playlist from sad songs
of heartbreak and anger to songs
that were about love and prayer,

or managed to stay sane while the world
was heartless and unforgiving and never
let you forget the time spent in the rain,

or avoided playing the same game that ruined
you for the thrill of getting blood pumping
in your veins,

or fell in love with a bee from a faraway place
that was never part of the plan but reminded
you of God's grace,

or focused on the cold embrace of stars in space
that twinkled against the infinite dark with
cadences too stellar contain in your little brain.

Despite the stark hardships
that were thrown your way,
the horrible words you heard
them say, the times the blue
sky looked too gray, the marks
they left with you to display,

you've managed to shake off the
bark and all its terrible weight,
created a place for your heart to
race in the comfort of loving arms,
replaced your hate with hope and
praise, and you'll continue to grow

each and every single day.

www.ingramcontent.com/pod-product-compliance
Lightning Source LLC
Chambersburg PA
CBHW030448100526
44580CB00002B/40